The Great Adoptee Search Book

The Great Adoptee Search Book

by
Jean A. S. Strauss

printed by the Heffernan Press
Worcester, Massachusetts

Published by
Castle Rock Publishing Company
Post Office Box 161, Worcester, MA 01602

Manufactured in the United States
of America

International Standard Book
Number: 0-9627982-2-3

TABLE OF CONTENTS

TO SEARCH OR NOT TO SEARCH...

People in America have many misconceptions about adoption. The general public often believes that adopted families aren't like "normal" biological families, that their relationships aren't as close as those bound by blood ties. Adoptive parents aren't looked upon as the child's "real" parents.

Birthparents are also misunderstood. It is a common belief that birth mothers give up their babies, get on with their lives, and never look back. Many assume the majority of birth mothers do <u>not</u> want to be "found".

Because of the above stereotypes, the idea of reuniting birth parents and birth children is often misinterpreted. People assume that adoptees who search are looking for their "real parents", that they are dissatisfied with their lives. Many believe adoptees are better off not knowing about their natural origins, or they really have no right to knowledge about their roots.

These presumptions are horribly flawed. Every human being deserves to know about their origins. In fact, to deny individuals this right is to cripple them. One's identity can only be fully developed through complete self-knowledge.

The reality is that an adoptee from a loving, nurturing home with parents that are loved unconditionally, can still feel incomplete. It is as if pieces are missing inside their souls. They simply do not know the truth about their origins. That knowledge is their birthright.

Today, more than ever, adult adoptees are seeking their natural origins. This process of self discovery has three parts: making the decision to search, the active search process, then coping with the outcome of those search efforts, be they "successful" or not.

That first step, making the initial decision to search, is extraordinarily personal. For some adoptees it is an easy choice. Driven by a strong need to learn about their natural heritage, they jump into a search without hesitation. Others may agonize over the decision for years. Plagued by doubt or guilt they ponder questions. How will this affect their parents? What if their natural parents don't want to be found? Until their need to know overcomes their fears, many adoptees are not yet ready to begin.

Whichever way the decision is ultimately arrived at, one characteristic is common among searchers: they don't just <u>want</u> to know about their origins, they <u>have</u> to know. They search because they <u>must</u>. It is this drive that sustains them throughout their quest.

Yet, once that intitial decision to search has been made, a perplexing question arises. Where does one begin to look?

How does one search for their biological roots? This book is designed to guide adoptees through the maze of paper and people who are the key to their puzzle.

THE 15 CARDINAL RULES OF SEARCHING

1. BELIEVE IN YOUR RIGHT TO KNOW ABOUT YOUR ORIGINS.

2. PROTECT THE PRIVACY OF PEOPLE YOU SEEK

3. BEGIN TO SEARCH ONLY IF YOU ARE OVER 18.

4. ASK THE RIGHT QUESTIONS.

5. ASSUME ANYTHING YOU'VE BEEN TOLD COULD BE WRONG.

6. KEEP RECORDS OF EVERYTHING.

7. REDUNDANCY OF INFORMATION HELPS ESTABLISH TRUTHS.

8. ALWAYS BE PREPARED. Plan ahead of time.

9. BE PATIENT. Don't jump to hasty conclusions.

10. THINK. Use your creativity.

11. REMEMBER YOU ARE NOT ALONE.

12. LEAVE NO STONE UNTURNED!

13. NEVER TAKE "NO" FOR AN ANSWER.

14. KNOW THYSELF. Know your expectations. Alter them if they are unrealistic.

15. NEVER ASSUME YOU ARE SEEKING PEOPLE WHO DON'T WANT TO BE FOUND. Your birth parents didn't seal your records - society did.

THE FORMULA FOR A SEARCH

Like most adoptees, when I began my search, I had no idea what to do. I was able to retrieve all the records my parents had kept on my adoption, but I didn't know how to use that information. It wasn't until I crossed paths with a former investigative reporter from LIFE magazine that I began to learn where and how to uncover clues.

But even with guidance, my initial investigation was awkward and turbulent. In the first months of my search, I rode an emotional rollercoaster. I went from high every time I found a new piece of information to low every time a door was closed in my face. I was putting so much pressure on each information source that I actually impeded my search. Like a rookie detective, I was nervous. I'd never done anything like this before. But my desperate attitude worked against me. I was an ineffective and unhappy sleuth.

Eventually I realized I was pursuing each lead as if my entire search hinged upon it. To hope to succeed, I had to change the way I approached searching. I needed a formula - something that would shift my focus away from <u>what</u> I was seeking to the process of <u>how</u> I was seeking it. The formula I eventually used helped me to locate my birthparents.

In essence, the formula is simply philosophically different from my initial method. I knocked on the same doors, but with a different goal.

The search is divided into three phases: Gathering, Profiling, and Cross-Referencing. This is how they work together to produce results.

Phase One

In the "Gathering" phase, the goal is to amass as much background information as possible. Seven major sources are used for research in this phase. These sources are simply the organizations and individuals who were involved in the events of your birth and adoption. They include your parents, the delivery physician, the hospital where you were born, the adoption agency, the attorney who represented your parents, the courts, and vital statistics offices which recorded your birth.

Phase Two

After accumulating as much information as possible from all seven sources, a PROFILE chart is created on each person being sought - both birth parents and other birth relatives. In essence, this is painting a picture of someone with words, albeit, often an incomplete picture.

Phase Three

After the profiles are created, active searching begins with cross-referencing and matching clues. Numerous other resources are utilized in this phase of the search; from the local library to government agencies to private individuals. With hard work and perseverance, cross-referencing will help you solve your puzzle.

By using this formula my search had a strategy to it, and that made me more poised when asking for information. I became an efficient hunter and searching actually became fun. Most important, I succeeded in unlocking the door to my origins.

It is now time to begin YOUR search.

PHASE ONE: GATHERING

THE SEARCH JOURNAL

Today, you start your search. To begin, you need two simple things: a three ring binder, and your amended birth certificate.

From day one, keep meticulous track of all the information that you gather. Whether in a binder, a journal, or a shoe box - every piece of paper, every clue, should be recorded and kept together.

Whatever cataloging system you use is not the issue. Documenting your search is. The tiniest clue found early on may be the link that solves your search years down the road. Take care to record every lead that you follow. Write down synopses of phone conversations and meetings. Xerox everything. Something seemingly insignificant may become the keystone of your efforts.

Be sure to keep copies of not only what you have received, but also what you yourself have <u>sent</u>. This will help you recall <u>who</u> you've contacted, <u>how</u> you've worded your request, and <u>when</u> it was sent. Such records will be invaluable for future correspondence and keeping track of your investigation.

Decide this very moment how and where you are going to organize your material. Then always make sure new research is cataloged immediately. From here on out, for the sake of giving it a title, this will be known as your search journal.

Now you are truly ready to begin. To know who you're looking for, you need to know a number of facts. Most importantly, you need to know a <u>name</u>.

Most searchers start out without knowing their given name at birth or the name of either birth parent. Whether you already know this information or not, proceed with this section. Contact the seven major sources in Phase One. Learn as much as you can about the background of your birth parents. This will help you not only to locate them, but to understand them and their circumstances. The more you know, the better prepared you are to make your first contact with your birth relatives.

HOW TO ASK FOR INFORMATION

Some people are born investigators. They ask for information without batting an eye, and are cool, calm and collected in every situation. Able to think quickly on their feet, they charm or finess information out of sources seemingly without effort.

Unfortunately, such characteristics were not in my repertoire when I began searching. I was unsure, hyper, and revealing. But over five years of searching, I learned a few good rules to follow when approaching people for information.

1. Believe in your right to know about your origins. Your attitude will inspire confidence in others, particularly sources.

2. Don't tell people you're searching for a birth parent unless you have to. Tell them you're doing genealogical research instead (which is also true!).

3. Always be friendly and courteous - even when someone does not respond in kind.

4. In a polite way, never take "NO" for an answer. Keep calling back, keep trying. Don't be neurotic about it, just calmly convince people that your need for information is not an idle request.

5. Be prepared. Always think through ahead of time how you are going to approach someone. Write it out, practice it in front of a mirror.

PARENTS

Some parents open the door before you have to ask, offering their assistance in any search efforts. Some go so far as to initiate a search themselves, sensing the information they find is important to their child. But other parents hesitate to even discuss the fact that their children are adopted (in fact, some adoptees never learn until they are adults that they <u>were</u> adopted...).

There's a range of scenarios in between these two extremes. Whatever your particular situation, the reality is that your parents may have information that can help you. If at all possible, confide in them. Not only can they provide information, they can provide emotional support.

As an aside, I was one of those adoptee searchers who chose not to include my own mother in my search efforts. I didn't because I thought I was protecting her. I was afraid she might misunderstand my motives. I was wrong. I wish now that I had shared with her my needs - she would have been supportive and I wouldn't have spent years feeling deceptive. Afterall, the reason I chose to search for my roots was to learn the <u>truth</u> about myself, to complete myself. To hide that need was, in essence, hypocritical.

Part of my fear had to do with our society's misconception (which we have already discussed) that adoptees search to locate their "real parents" (I loathe the media's overuse of this label). The reality is that most adoptees who search do so not to find parents, but to find <u>themselves</u>. The need to have a complete self history, which drives many <u>non</u>-adoptees to do geneological research, is not that different from an adoptee's need to find their own roots.

Most parents will ultimately understand this need. That doesn't mean that the thought of their child searching won't cause them some anxiety. The system of adoption in this country is shrouded in secrecy. It is the unknown that people fear. There exists a common worry among adoptive parents that the arrival of a birth parent into their child's life will replace their role as parent, or somehow diminish it. An interesting outcome of many searches, however, is that the reunion with birth parents can further soldify the relationship between the adoptive parents - the "real parents" - and their son or daughter.

If your parents are willing to help in your search, ask them to gather together all the documents they have from your adoption. Their paperwork may include a background history on you from the adoption agency (unless your adoption was handled independently through an attorney). They may have forms filled out by a foster parent who was responsible for your care before placement. And, most importantly, they will probably have the Final Decree for Adoption.

THE FINAL DECREE

The Final Decree is the document issued by the court granting parents permanent custody of the adopted child. This is issued at the end of a probationary period and legally finalizes the adoption. Most parents will keep a copy of this document because it proves the adopted child is legally theirs.

The Decree is important to you as a searcher because of one vital piece of information: it should tell you YOUR ORIGINAL NAME.

Unless you were abandoned and your parents never located (in which case you might be listed as "Baby Jane Doe"), you were probably given at least a last name when you were relinquished. And many birth mothers will give their child a complete name. Sometimes, this full name carries hidden clues. The first or middle name you were given may have been the name of one of your birth parents, or the name of a grandparent.

Having the last name alone is a great coup. If you can learn what the marital status of your birth mother was at the time of your birth, it may indicate whether the last name you were given was hers or your birth father's (single mothers almost always give the child their own last name).

Another document your parents may have is the PETITION TO ADOPT. This legal paper is the formal request to the court by your parents that they be granted adoption. Like the Final Decree, this document should have your original name, birthdate and place. It also may contain your birth mother's full name and address. Parents are less likely to have received a copy of this, but sometimes they do. You won't know uless you ask.

If for some reason your parents no longer have a copy of either the Petition to Adopt or the Final Decree, the attorney who represented your parents in the adoption may still have a copy on file. The attorney's office might not be willing to release a copy to you, but they should to their clients - your parents. Enlist them to help you, if you can.

Another way to retrieve the Final Decree is through the Adoptions Clerk in the county where your adoption was finalized legally. Write a short, businesslike note to the Clerk asking them to search their files and records for your adoption record. Tell them that you would like to be furnished with certified copies of both the interlocutory order of adoption and the final order of adoption. You will, of course, need to tell them your adoptive name, date of birth, and date of adoption, as well as your parents (adoptive) names. Contact the county administrative office or the State Adoption Regulating Unit to learn where and to whom you should direct your request.

WAIVER OF CONFIDENTIALITY

You will find that agencies and individuals are more supportive if you have your parents' support. One document that you can "create" which will be quite helpful to you throughout your search is a Waiver of Confidentiality. Many adoption agencies have their own waiver forms, and state Departments of Social Services may have one on file which you can use. If necessary, you could create your own. Use the example on the following page as a guide. Whatever form you use, it will need to be signed by both you and your adoptive parents in front of a notary.

Once you have your Waiver of Confidentiality, carry it with you whenever you meet with someone in connection with your search. Most people are much more comfortable in assisting your efforts if they understand you have the blessing of your parents.

Make sure you give a copy to the agency which handled your adoption, and to the lawyer who assisted your parents. On the outside chance that your birth mother or birth father are trying to locate you, the agency will need a waiver on file for you to make a reunion possible.

WAIVER OF RIGHTS TO CONFIDENTIALITY
ADOPTION RECORDS

AGENCY CASE NUMBER
STATE CASE NUMBER

PLEASE NOTE:

This form must be witnessed by the Department or a licensed adoption agency representative or notarized. If the signing of this form is witnessed by the Department or an agency representative, some form of identification of the person signing must be obtained and noted on this form.

DESIGNATE ONE

☐ Birth Parent
☐ Adult Adoptee
☐ Adoptive Parent(s)

PART A. *To be completed by person signing waiver.*

By signing this form, I voluntarily and knowingly waive my rights to the confidentiality of adoption records maintained by the State Department of Social Services or licensed adoption agency for the sole purpose of allowing the Department or licensed adoption agency to arrange for contact with the following persons as designated:

☐ The Birth Parent   ☐ The Adoptee   ☐ The Adoptive Parent(s)

I realize that all of the designated persons, i.e., the birth parent, the adult adoptee, and the adoptive parent(s) (if living) must sign a waiver before the agency may arrange for contact among these persons, and that signing this waiver does not necessarily insure that a contact can be arranged. I understand that the law prohibits the Department or licensed adoption agency from soliciting, directly or indirectly, the execution of such a waiver.

I understand that I should keep the adoption agency informed of my correct name and address. If I decide to rescind this waiver, I will notify the Department or adoption agency in writing.

SIGNATURE				DATE
ADDRESS	CITY	STATE	ZIP CODE	TELEPHONE NUMBER
OTHER NAME(S) BY WHICH I HAVE BEEN KNOWN		IDENTIFICATION *(SPECIFY, I.E., DRIVER'S LICENSE, PASSPORT, ETC.)* *(COMPLETE THIS ITEM IF PART B IS COMPLETED.)*		

PART B. *To be completed by licensed adoption agency representative. If Part B is completed, do not complete Part C.*

SIGNATURE OF ADOPTION AGENCY REPRESENTATIVE	DATE	TELEPHONE NUMBER
AGENCY DEPARTMENT NAME	ADDRESS	

PART C. *To be completed by a Notary Public only if Part B is not completed.*

State of _____

County of _____ } ss.

Before me, _____, a Notary Public in and for said County and

State, personally appeared _____, known to me to be the person whose name is subscribed to the within instrument, and acknowledged that he/she executed the same.

IN WITNESS WHEREOF, I have hereunto set my hand and affixed my official seal this _____

day of _____ , 19 _____ .

(Affix Notarial Seal)

Notary Public in and for the County of _____

State of _____

My commission expires _____

15

THE AMENDED BIRTH CERTIFICATE

The easiest document to retrieve, and one you should include immediately in your search journal, is your birth certificate - a piece of paper your parents received when their adoption of you was made final. If you do not have a copy of your birth certificate, you can get a new one by writing to the county or state office of Vital Statistics where you were born. It is the only document to which everyone will agree you have a right!

Once the certificate is in your hands, take a close look at it. You have perhaps had access to it all your life, yet never realized it holds clues that can help you learn your original identity.

It is an amended version, of course. Your original birth certificate, issued shortly after your birth, was sealed upon your adoption. Certain obvious changes are made on the amended birth certificate: the names of your birth parents, their ages and states of birth are all removed and replaced with your adoptive parents names. The name you were given at birth is also changed. But the rest of the information is usually intact. Your birth date, the exact time of your birth, the hospital or location where you were born, the city and county, and the name of the physician or attendant who delivered you are generally listed.

These clues will lead you into your past.

THE PHYSICIAN

The odds are, you were delivered by a physician in a hospital. Locating that person who delivered you can be a key to your mystery. Even if a delivery physician doesn't remember your birth mother (and chances are, he won't), he may have <u>medical records</u> on file which will have the name and old address of your birth mother.

Doctors are easy to find. The first place to look, obviously, is through the hospital where you were born. If the doctor no longer works there, the hospital administration may know where he/she is practicing currently. There are also other avenues to try. Your local library might have a copy of <u>Who's Who in American Medicine</u> or the <u>AMA Medical Directory</u> in the reference section. These list almost every licensed physician in the country, and will give you the most current addresses for them.

If you strike out at the library, contact the Medical Quality Assurance Board or the Board of Medical Examiners in the state of your birth (usually these are located in the state capital). Call or write them and ask for your doctor's license number and a copy of his license file. Mid-wives are also licensed by state, so if your birth was attended by a mid-wife and not a physician, the Board may help you to locate him. If you are able to locate the doctor through either of these sources, you should learn the following: when they graduated from medical school, and where their current practice is located.

If your doctor graduated from medical school only shortly before you were born, he was probably an intern or resident while in attendance at your birth. If this is the case, he most likely will not have any personal medical records concerning you. However, if he had been in practice for a while, he may have maintained records on both you and your birth mother.

Whatever the case, if you can locate the physician who delivered you, contact him. Even if no records on you are available, the physician might be willing to assist you in your search. Each person has their own opinion about reuniting adoptees and birth parents. Some people will be very helpful. Others will treat you as if you are doing something criminal. You won't know until you ask.

Ask your physician to write to the hospital where you were born for records. Of course, a name will be required and that may present a problem. You may find as you search that the old axiom "which comes first, the chicken or the egg?" applies to an adoptee's search. If you had the name, you could ask for the record. If you had the record, you could learn the name. Hopefully, you have been able to locate a copy of your Final Decree and from that have at least a last name to use.

COUNTY RECORDS

What else is on your birth certificate that can help you? Lots of information.

Take your birth date. You know the time and date of your birth, as well as the city and county where you were born. Even if you were born in New York City, there are a finite number of people born there on a given day.

Most counties have a recorder's or registrar's office. These generally keep duplicates on file of all birth certificates for people born within the county borders.

Visit the recorder's office in person if it is at all possible. Recorders keep books or microfilm which list births in numerical sequence by birth date. So, if you know your birthdate, you should be able to see the names of all babies born in the county on that given day.

Xerox or copy down the list of names. Your own name might not be listed there (the name you've grown up with). That's because you might be listed by the name given to you at birth.

Look up each birth certificate (for your own gender) that has your birthdate. Write down all the information you find on each person (parents names, delivery physician, hospital, etc.), and catalog this into your search journal. If you come across a birth certificate that is completely blanked out except for the name, chance's are you have just located your given name at birth (unless you come from a huge county like Los Angeles where more than one adoptee may have been born on the same day).

But perhaps no certificates are blanked out, and your own name was not among those listed. Is one of those recorded births your own? Do any seem to match your amended birth certificate - same doctor, same hospital? You may be extraordinarily lucky and have found your original birth certificate which was mistakenly not "sealed" by the county. If so, you not only have your own birth name, but your birth parents' names and addresses.

There is another way to establish which name may be your own. Using the information you have gotten via the county recorder's office, send off for the birth certificate for each person on the list. The one certificate which doesn't come back is your own - it was sealed at the time of your adoption. Again, if you come from a large county, there may be more than one sealed birth certificate for a given date. But this will at least give you a short list from which to begin.

THE ADOPTION AGENCY

Many adoption agencies will share as much information as possible - outside of names and addresses - with adult adoptees. In fact some agencies, with the consent of all three parties of the adoption triangle, will assist in facilitating a reunion. On rare occasions, social workers may actually initiate contact with a birth parent to see if they are willing to be reunited with a birth child.

In the last two decades, agencies have become more sensitive to the strong needs of adoptees to contact their roots. They generally try to complete as much of the "picture" as they can for the adoptee. But, as a rule, most are unwilling to release any identifying information. Some social workers feel honor-bound not to do so. Others are restricted by law.

The agency which handled your adoption may have provided your parents a background history on you at the time of your adoption. This report usually includes a description of physical characteristics such as height, weight, hair color, eye color, complexion and age of one or both birth parents. Some will list the birthdate and place of birth of a birth parent. Nationalities, religion, occupation, and education may also be divulged. Most agencies try to provide as detailed a medical history of birthparents as possible (though most birth parents tend to be young and fairly healthy). Written in the report may be a synopsis of the events surrounding your conception and birth. Sometimes this information may have been informally relayed to your parents through a conversation with a social worker. Ask your parents to try to remember specific facts they were told by the agency.

If you are able to locate this background report through your parents, should you still attempt to contact the adoption agency? By all means. More information might be relayed - either facts omitted from the report at the time of your adoption or events which might have occurred since.

For example, I already had a background report from my parents, but I contacted the agency which handled my adoption anyway. They informed me that my birth mother had written to them when I was five years old inquiring about my well being. She wrote that she had married shortly after I was born, and that she had four children. They had heard nothing from her since. But this information gave me both confidence that my birth mother wanted to know what had happened to me, and inspiration that I had half-siblings to find as well. The agency's repetition of the information my parents had been given further substantiated what I already knew about myself.

Agencies can be reluctant to share information with an adoptee who is actively searching for a birth parent. Because of this, it is wise to couch any request for information in vague terms. Don't ask for your birth parents names up front. Let them know that you are very curious about your background, and that you hope they will help you fill in the blanks (which is the truth!). Give them as much information about yourself as possible so that they will be able to locate your file: your birth date, your original name (if you know it), your Social Service case number (from the agency paperwork your parents may have), the court order number (from the Final Decree), your parents' names and address at the time of your adoption.

Follow up this information with every question you can think of. Are there photographs of your birth parents on file? If not, is there any written description of them? How old were your birth parents? Where were they born? Where were their families from originally? Had they gone to high school or college? What were they like? What were they interested in? What did they do for a living? Is anything known about natural grandparents or other blood relatives? Is there any information regarding their medical histories of which you should be aware? Do you have any siblings? What was the religion of your birth parents? What happened that your birth mother needed to relinquish you for adoption?

Think up as many questions as you hope they have answers for, and also ask questions about things you already may know. Again, if the agency answers correspond with information you already know, that helps to further confirm you are on the right track. REDUNDANCY OF INFORMATION HELPS ESTABLISH TRUTHS.

You may prefer to do any initial contact with the agency through the mail. If you do, then call the agency first and ask where to direct your inquiry. This saves time and makes sure the right person receives your request.

Except in rare instances, agencies will answer such inquiries. Don't be disappointed if all you find out is what you already knew. Again, every confirmation helps to establish facts.

After several weeks, you may want to follow up their response with a thank you letter. Perhaps use this opportunity to ask about the possibility of a reunion. Would the agency help facilitate this if your adoptive parents sign a Waiver of Confidentiality? Can they assist you with any further information? Would they be willing to try to contact your birth mother to see if she is interested in a reunion?

Let them know the reasons you want to locate your birth mother or father. And, use your own intuition when making such an inquiry. Has the agency seemed helpful so far? Is there a way you can couch your request so that they might respond more readily? Should you wait longer, establish a better contact, before asking the agency for help?

As with any personal contact in your search, luck may have something to do with your outcome. Maybe you talked to someone on a good day, or a bad day. Out of the blue, a clerk or a social worker might let a piece of information slip.

Knowing someone is holding all the information you want and need right in front of them, and then having them withhold it from _you_ can be extraordinarily frustrating. Every adoptee who searches feels that frustration at some point or another. When it happens, try to maintain your composure. ALWAYS BE COURTEOUS AND APPRECIATIVE. That keeps the door open for another day, not only for you but for others searching as well.

Whatever the outcome with the adoption agency, hopefully you have new information to add to the profile of the people you seek. You may not have names yet. But the more information you gain about them can help you find their names elsewhere.

ATTORNEYS

The amount of involvement of an attorney in your adoption depends on whether you were adopted independently or through an agency. If you were placed through an agency, the attorney will have records only of the Petition to Adopt and the Final Decree. If it was an independent adoption, he may have much more (the Original Birth Certificate, the Surrender of Parental Rights, records of the financial arrangements, etc.).

Your parents were the clients that the attorney served, so, if possible, they should be included in any attempt to retrieve information from the law office. At the very least, as was suggested earlier, bring along a Waiver of Confidentiality if you can.

Make an appointment with the attorney and offer to pay for his time. Any fees for an office visit may ultimately be waived, but this approach makes your request more formal and professional.

Whenever you have contact with an individual, your potential success in gaining information will rest somewhat on that individual's personal value system. Even though there may not be any laws restricting an attorney from providing information to you about your adoption, if they personally disagree with an adoptees right to search, you have no power to force them to do so. Hopefully, your parents law firm will share with you any and all documents maintained in their files.

ORIGINAL BIRTH CERTIFICATES

Attempt to get your original birth certificate. Every so often, a clerk will accidentally not seal a record. It is not unknown for an adoptee to receive their original birth certificate simply by writing to their state Bureau of Vital Statistics and requesting a full copy.

The key to receiving an original birth certificate is using your original name. Most states require the following information: your name (original), the date of your birth and the city where you were born, and both your mother's and father's full names.

Write a short letter to the Bureau of Vital Statistics, and use only the information you know are facts. Your birthdate and time, the county and hospital, and the attending physician are all things you already know. By now, you may know your original birth name. Perhaps you only know your last name. Write only your last name out. If you know your full name, obviously use it. If you know either birth parents name, include that. Find out what fees are necessary, and mail your request in with a money order (don't use a personal check! - it has the wrong name...).

The odds are that you will receive a notice from the state that they are unable to locate your birth certificate or that they need further information. But the chance that you might get lucky, is worth the time it takes to send the request. You could learn a lot of key information! (Names and addresses.)

HOSPITAL RECORDS

Retrieving records from a hospital is not easy. But, recent laws in some states have made access to personal medical records less difficult. If anything, you may learn a few small clues regarding your delivery. Anything to add to your profile portfolio is worth pursuing. And, like with your original birth certificate, you just might get lucky.

Hospitals will usually keep a file on both you and your birth mother. There will be a record of your birth mother's admittance to the hospital. It will have your birth mother's name and address and possibly her phone number. There will be a Certificate of Live Birth which will also contain this information, as well as much of the information which is on your birth certificate. A "Newborn Record" is a recording of your physical examination at birth as well as at the time of your discharge from the hospital. If there were complications, this may be more than a one page report. Your birth mother's name will also be on this report. Also, sometimes a copy of the Social Welfare form authorizing a social worker to pick up the baby from the hospital may be in the file. Again, this form will have your birth mother's name and signature on it.

Call the hospital records department and learn what procedures are necessary to obtain a copy of your medical file. Obviously, use your original name and don't tell them that you're adopted and searching for your birth mother... It is not outside the realm of reasonableness for an individual who was born at a hospital to also request their mother's medical record from the birth also. This is a particularly logical request to come from a young woman in her "child-bearing years".

Fill out the necessary forms, and make the request in your original name. A small problem arises at this time. Most hospitals may require that your signature be notarized on the form. At this point, you may need to find an ally who will notarize your signature of your original name. This is a "gray area". Notaries are generally honest people. At issue here is whether or not use of your original name is dishonest. It is, afterall, "your name". It was given to you at birth. And the information you seek is about your own birth. It is a question that is open to interpretation. You hopefully will locate a notary who is sympathetic to your cause.

Another approach may prove more successful. Where hospital records clerks may view your personal request for records with suspicion, they will not question such a request from a doctor. If you can enlist the help of your own physician, or even the doctor who performed your delivery, they may be able to retrieve your medical records without hesitation.

APPEAL TO THE COURTS

If you have had no luck learning information from any of the above sources, then there is one more thing you can try: appeal to the courts to open your records.

The first thing to do is to become familiar with the adoption laws in your state (the state where your adoption took place). If your local library is large enough, copies of the State's Statutes and Codes books should be available in the Reference section. If none are on hand, check with your librarian to see if you can order a copy through the interlibrary loan system. Is there a college in your area with a law school? If your local library doesn't have the books you need, a college law library would have them in their stacks. If you are unable to locate any legal texts in local libraries, contact a local law firm. They will definitely have the resources you seek. Failing that, there's generally a law library in the state capital. Establish a contact via phone or mail and have them mail you photocopies of the information you need. Libraries are usually very helpful, and their fees for photocopying and mailing are not expensive.

What laws are you looking for? Those statutes that pertain to adoption law both when you were adopted and now, and any case reports that regard the unsealing of adoption records. In other words, learn what decisions have been made by the courts in your state regarding opening the records of an adoptee.

Are records opened only when a medical emergency warrants it? Or are there other instances when records are unsealed? Are there circumstances involved similar to your own? Could there be? Is there a specific form that must be filed in your petition to open your own records?

Learn as much as you can before you begin the petition process. Some adoptees have had success with informally contacting a judge before filing a petition. Some judges are sympathetic to an adoptee's plea to learn about their roots. Everything is worth a try. Explain why you need to learn about yourself. If your parents have signed a Waiver of Confidentiality, include that as a part of your plea. If you are unsuccessful in either a written or in-person plea with a judge, then hire a lawyer and file a formal petition with the courts.

If you are successful with either your informal or formal plea, you will have succeeded in gathering all the information you need for the next phase of your search: profiling the people you seek.

PHASE TWO: PROFILE BUILDING

Depending upon your own circumstances, you by now have either a lot of information or seemingly little. But even without that all important original birth name, you hopefully have enough information to profile your birthparents.

Who were they? Where were they from? What did they look like? What interests did they have? What did they do for a living?

Using the sample chart on the following page, create a profile on both your birth mother and birth father. Make charts on other birth relatives as well if you have been able to learn anything about them. Review every piece of information that you have cataloged in your search journal. Reread each line, each word, for possible clues. Is there anything you might have missed? Fill in as many blanks as you can and create new areas for information that you may have which the sample chart doesn't contain.

Now, look carefully at the chart for your birth mother. If you have her name, and/or an old address, you have a lot to go on. But perhaps the opposite is your case. You don't have much. Let's say you only know a physical description of her, and a few other meager clues. Your profile chart has blank spaces.

Don't despair! I <u>never</u> knew an exact name. I had a description, an occupation, and a birth date. And I was able to find my birth mother. It does happen.

THE PROFILE CHART

_____
Name

_____   _____
Birthdate   Birthplace

_____   _____
Age at your birth   _____
                            Last Known Address

_____
Marital Status

Height:_____   Weight:_____

Eye Color:_____   Hair Color:_____

Religion:_____   Race:_____

Citizenship:_____
Nationality(s):_____ _____

_____
Educational Background

_____
Medical History

_____
Military Service

Background History:_____

_____
_____

If you feel you have been crafty and clever to date in your search, you are right. But now the search becomes truly creative. Use your own genius to cross match clues and lead you closer to your goal.

As you fill in your charts, ask yourself as many questions as you can about these people. Establish new catagories of information that fit your circumstances. Be CREATIVE. Try to envision in your mind an image of the people you are looking for and the paths in life they may have followed since your birth.

Armed with whatever information you now have, you are ready to Cross-Reference. You are now searching for a person.

Where do you look next? Take your search journal and your wits and make haste to your local library.

PHASE THREE: CROSS-REFERENCING

FACT: THE PEOPLE YOU ARE SEEKING HAVE THEIR NAMES IN PRINT SOMEWHERE. ALL YOU HAVE TO DO IS FIND THEM THROUGH THE PROCESS OF ELIMINATION....

Whether in phone books, newpapers, records, directories, class lists, or driver's licenses, everybody ends up on paper somewhere. As you move forward in your search, you try to zero in on a specific person. To do that you CROSS-REFERENCE one or more clues to piece your puzzle together.

LIBRARIES

A powerful place to begin this exercise is at the local library. The use of libraries has already been discussed in the sections on physicians and attorneys. As you begin to cross-reference, the true value of a library to your search will become more and more evident.

Trips to the library may not have titillated you in the past, but that's about to change. Your whole mystery can be unlocked within a library's stacks. There are so many resources at your disposal. And no one at a library is ever going to say, "no, you can't see that...".

A good central library will have all the reference materials you need to begin. If you aren't familiar with how to use a library or how to find specific information, librarians can be among the most helpful people on earth. You may find yourself working in tandem with a librarian in your hometown, and a librarian a thousand miles away in the home county of your birth mother.

Research with a library through the mail is entirely plausible, effective, and practical.

A local library with an interlibrary loan system is a fabulous extension to other libraries throughout the country. If your particular hometown library does not have a certain book you need, or a newspaper on microfilm from a different area, borrow it from another library via an interlibrary loan.

There are many speciality libraries across the country (geneology libraries, law libraries, medical libraries, etc.). To learn what's available to you, check the <u>American Library Directory</u> in the reference section. You may be surprised by the number of resources available to you in your area.

What's in a library?

CITY DIRECTORIES

Do you have a possible last name for a birth parent (from your own original name) but no <u>first</u> name to know exactly who you're looking for? Or do you have an old address or phone number as a clue, but no name?

Most cities publish or have published city directories. These terrific resources list residents in three ways: by the resident's NAME, by PHONE NUMBER, and by STREET ADDRESSES.

Local libraries will have city directories for the surrounding area. If you're interested in a directory for a city from out-of-state but are unable to travel there in person, call a local library in that city. Librarians are generally willing to do research for you over the phone for nominal fees (usually just the cost of copying and mailing)

A city directory may tell you:

Name(s) of residents
Address and whether the resident
  rents or owns the property
Telephone number
Marital Status of resident
Occupation
Place of Business

Also directories may give forwarding addresses of residents who have moved in the previous year. This is invaluable for tracking someone to new locations.

**There is a "directory" of city directories in the U.S. called... <u>City and Business Directories of the United</u>

<u>States</u> which may be helpful if you're trying to learn what directories exist for an area.

How can you use a directory to <u>cross reference</u> information and lead you to a person?

Let's say you know your original birth name through your Final Decree. If you know a location - a town - where your birth mother may have resided, begin by looking there in the appropriate year(s). Perhaps your birth mother was too young to have been employed, but you know what your maternal grandfather was a clock maker. Armed with a directory for the year <u>before</u> your birth, look under the heading for your original last name. Can you find any individuals who were clock makers? You may have located your birth grandfather. Obviously, if your birth mother (or father) had an <u>occupation</u>, you would check them in this way also.

Make a list of any names that might fit.

Now, track those individuals forwards and backwards through different years. For example, if you locate an individual with the same last name and occupation as your birth mother in a directory a year or two before your birth, does she disappear the year of your birth? Does she reappear a few years down the road? Did she exist five years before your birth or ten? Would this fit the description of your birth mother? Let's say your birth mother was 21 when you were born and you are told she was a store clerk. You find a store clerk with the same last name in the city directory - but cross-referencing backward you find the person was also listed in the city directory ten years before your birth (when your birth mother would have been 11...). Obviously, the store clerk in the directory could not have been your birth mother.

In this way, can you narrow down a list of names to one single person? If so, where did she live? Can you tell if she owned or rented the residence?

Using the directory section which indexes by addresses, who were her neighbors in the year of your birth? Do they still exist? (Track them through subsequent city directories or phone books.)

Do people exist that you can locate who may have known this woman? A landlord perhaps, or a neighbor? Is her place of employment listed? Does the company still exist today? Does anyone working there remember your birth mother? Are personnel records maintained in an office?

If you think you have found a potential match, track her through subsequent years. Did she move? Did she suddenly disappear? Could that mean she married? Mark down in your journal that you need to check for marriage records or announcements for those particular years.

You can try tracing every person you're looking for if you know their last name, or an old address, or an old phone number. Try to narrow down a list of names for your birth mother - her parents - your birth father - his parents.

Similar to city directories are Cole's Directories. These are helpful if you have an old address but no phone number or name. Cole's publications are available for most areas of the United States. If you find one in your library, but need one for a different area, there should be a phone number inside the cover for a local sales office where you might access other Cole Directories.

** A word of caution about city directories. They are excellent resources, but be aware that it can sometimes take time for data to be updated. Information on a given individual isn't always complete in each issue. Be sure to check a span of years instead of just one single year to avoid missing a key listing.

MAPS

Being able to visualize the area you're looking in can be extremely helpful. Get maps of the town where you were born, the place where both birth parents were born, and the place where you believe they might be today. Your library will have atlases that can assist you. Another resource is the automobile club.

If you know addresses, locate the streets your birth parents lived on. Locate where they worked. Notice the surrounding towns, and the names of adjoining counties. Become as familiar as possible with the target area.

When divers do an underwater search, they begin where they expect to find an object and anchor a rope in that spot. Then they slowly and meticulously swim a spiral out from the center until they locate the object of their search. This saves them time and energy, and also keeps them from missing what they seek.

Searching for a person is done in a similar fashion. Begin where "you" started and in the regions where your birthparents were from and spiral out, checking each surrounding town and county for records.

** TIP: If in your search you travel out of town to hunt down records, map out everywhere you want to go and everything you wish to accomplish ahead of time. You don't want to make an expensive trip twice. In addition, be sure to make appointments in advance if you're planning to visit an organization or individuals in person.

PROFILE THE TOWN

What was the town like where you were born in the year of your birth? What is it like today? What about the area where your birth mother was from? Your birth father?

Using the resources available in both your local library and the chambers of commerce in those cities where you focus your search efforts, develop a profile of the regions where you and your birth parents originated.

What industry exists? What's the population of the area? What schools, what churches, and what hospitals are there? Where is the county seat? How many libraries are there? And what are people like from the region? Are they predominantly middle class? Catholic, Jewish, WASP? Liberal or conservative?

Knowing more about where you're looking serves two purposes: it enhances your knowledge of your own roots and provides insight into where to look.

For example, let's say you know your birth mother was from Kensington, Kentucky. You also know that she was 17 years old when you were born, that her family was Catholic, and that her father was a farm laborer. If you grew up in Chicago, you might not know much about Kensington.

Through research, you learn that Kensington is primarily conservative, that the prime industry is horse breeding, that families tended to be upper class, and the majority were White Anglo-Saxon Protestants. You now have a much clearer vision of the world your birth mother lived in, and a better understanding of her life.

Profiling a town or region won't necessarily give you specific clues (although it can). It definitely <u>will</u> give you a sense of time, place and circumstance. Use it to broaden your knowledge of your past and an understanding of the people to whom you're biologically related.

One resource your local library may have, or you may be able to access through interlibrary loan is the <u>Consolidated Bibliography of County Histories in 50 States in 1961</u> written by Clarence Stewart Peterson. There are other volumes and encyclopedias on specific regions. Also, the Automobile Association of America (AAA) in addition to providing you maps can be a source of travel information about specific areas that can be useful in filling out your regional profile.

NEWSPAPERS

When you were born, your arrival was probably not listed in the birth announcement section of the newpaper. But when your birth parents were born (unless they were adopted also) it's possible their births were announced in their local paper.

If you know approximately <u>when</u> and <u>where</u> your birth parents were born, or if you have an exact date but no name, newspaper birth announcements are a great resource.

What does a birth announcement tell you? The baby's name, birth date, the parents' names, and sometimes their address. That's a lot!

How do you find what newspapers existed in the town of your birth parent's birth? Reference sections of most libraries will have the <u>State Union List of Newspapers</u>. There are other resources for finding newspapers and periodicals. Ask your librarian for help.

Once you know which newspaper you want, all you have to do is get microfilm copies to search through. Many are available on loan through local library collections. Usually, newspapers are filmed in one month or three month sections. It depends on the size of the paper, of course. The *New York Times* takes up a lot more space than a small local paper. Every single page of the paper is included.

This search process can be at once both tedious and fascinating. The advertisements from decades past can be quite entertaining. And, as you scan the pages, you will learn much about both the <u>era</u> and <u>area</u>.

There are three main records which newspapers keep: birth and marriage announcements, and obituaries. They all tend to be in the same section. Some papers only announce births on one day of the week. See if your paper follows any such pattern - it will save you time.

BIRTH ANNOUNCEMENTS

Realize it can take months for an announcement to appear. For this reason, you should check several months after the date you are trying to confirm. Let's say you know your birth mother was born on July 1, 1937 in Philadelphia, Pennsylvania, but you don't know her name. You would want to make a list of all baby girls born on July 1 in Philadelphia, and to be safe, check a period of several months.

With that list of names, cross reference a city directory of the area where you believe your mother lived when you were conceived or born. Do any names match up? For example, if there are twenty baby girls born in Philadelphia on July 1, 1937, and you know you were born in Seattle, Washington, do any of those twenty names show up in the Seattle city directory or phone book in the year preceding or following your birth?

Another way to use birth announcements from newspapers would be if you don't have a birthdate for your birth mother, but you know your original last name from your Final Decree. Let's say it was DUTTON. You also know that your birth mother was born in Topeka, Kansas and that she was 20 years old when you were born. If you were born on May 19, 1950, that would mean your birth mother had to have been born between May of 1929 and May of 1931. You would have to check local Topeka papers for a two and a half year period (from May of 1929 to December of 1931) looking for the annoucement of any baby girl born with the last name DUTTON. * Again, make copies of any names you find for your search journal. Then begin cross referencing with other sources. REMEMBER - birth mothers frequently give their birth children first and middle names that have meaning. Whether it is their own name, or the name of a birth relative your original first and middle name could be a significant clue.

MARRIAGE ANNOUNCEMENTS

Finding your birth mother's maiden name is a huge clue. Unfortunately, it might not leave a trail that you can follow very far.   She probably married at least once between your birth and today. But there are a number of ways to find out what her new name might be. Some involve meticulous searching of marriage, divorce, and death records.

Like birth announcements, marriage announcements give very helpful information: parents names and even addresses, and most importantly, the last name of the groom. Also, marriage announcements frequently include a picture of the bride and groom. For many adoptees, to possess a picture of a birth parent is a huge connection with their past.

If you have an idea of when and where a birth parent may have married, scanning through several years of newspapers for marriage or engagement announcements might produce results.

OBITUARIES

Obituaries are another resource, although one which searchers seem to avoid.   But obituaries and death records contain a lot of information worth pursuing.

If you have traced a birth grandparent, for example, through city directories up to 1967 and then the grandparent disappears, one of two things must have happened: either the grandparent moved away or died.

Check the local paper for a five year period - remember, city directories may take a year or two to catch up on current information - and check every obituary page. If you are "lucky" enough to locate your grandparent this way, the obituary might contain a short history of their life AND a list of their next of kin. Let's say your birth mother's maiden name was Lois Ann Smithe. You have never have been able to discover her married name. A typical obituary will give it to you as, "...survived by two daughters, Pauline Smithe of Belmont, and Lois Ann Greer of Las Cruces, New Mexico." Obviously, this sentence could lead you straight to your birth mother.

Be creative in your use of old newspapers as a resource. The results can be far-reaching!

THE COUNTY RECORDER

The County Recorder's office was already discussed in an earlier section on birth records. Counties keep keep other records as well: marriage, divorce, and death certificates.

As mentioned above, knowing your birth mother's maiden name is only the first step in locating her. You need to know who she is today. Chances are she's been going by a married name for years. There's also a chance that she married more than once.

Just like using records from newspapers, the county recorder's office can help you discover what name your birth mother may now be using. If you have an idea where and approximately when she married, and if you have a birth date, the recorders office or State Vital Statistics office will usually do a search for you. They will generally search only a five year period, and a fee will be charged for their services. If you do not have enough information to go on (ie. no birth date), you may have to do your searching in person at the local recorder's office.

County marriage records are usually listed alphabetically by both the bride's and groom's names. You may have to check records for every county in the state, or several possible states before you find a match.

Marriage records will show a great deal of information: full name, birth date, place of birth, parents names, and current addresses for both the bride and groom, plus the names of two witnesses. (As marriages are usually witnessed by close friends of the bride and groom, even if the married couple no longer lives in the area, perhaps a witness still does and knows the whereabouts of a birth parent.)

Obviously, if you locate a marriage certificate for your birth mother, you now have strong new information to aid your search. You also have new questions to answer.

Do she and her husband still live in the same city? County? State? The first thing to do is call information and see if your birthmother and her spouse are listed. If not, could they have returned to the city where her husband was born? Or where your birth mother was born or raised? Can you find the husband in an old city directory? Who did he work for? Does an old employer remember him? Where did he live? Does an old landlord or neighbor remember him? Do they know where he might have moved to? REMEMBER: to get the right answers you need to ask the right questions.

Finding a birth mother's married name should lead you much closer to making contact. One thing needs to be considered, however: she may have been widowed, divorced, or remarried. Check the divorce records in the same county where you found the marriage record.

Divorce records are usually filed alphabetically, so this shouldn't take too much additional time. Divorce records, like marriage records, will give you new information - possible new addresses, whether your birth mother reverted to her maiden name, names of children, etc.

Like an obituary, death certificates are valuable to locate. Do you have an idea where either set of birth grandparents might have lived? Check county recorder death records for grandparents. Like an obituary, these records should state the next of kin (and possibly give you a birth parents married name) and their address.

A word of caution. Don't jump to hasty conclusions! If you locate a name that on first view looks promising, don't run to the telephone to call them up. It is important to first gather as much information as possible before initiating contact. Find facts to support other facts. As difficult as it may be at times, proceed slowly and methodically. Searching carries an enormous responsibility. You need to find the right person. Discretion is both wise and considerate.

OTHER LIBRARY RESOURCES:

SURNAME BOOKS

Do you know a <u>nationality</u> of a birth parent but no last name, and then a list of names that are possibilites but you don't know their national origin? Books like <u>A Dictionary of Surnames</u> published by the Oxford Press can help sort out which names are Swedish versus Norweigian or Danish, which names are English versus Irish, which are Russian versus Polish.

This resource can be helpful in confirming a possible name.   Let's say you know that your birth mother's nationality was French and you have found a woman named Jane Boehke which fits the description of who you're looking for.   What nationality is Boehke? German. That's helpful to know. If a nationality and a name don't match, <u>don't</u> let that cancel out a good lead. Continue to follow it with the knowledge that one of your clues doesn't fit. You need to know MORE.

**Another word of caution. Information you are given isn't always correct. For instance, I was told by my adoption agency that my birth father was Norweigian, which in fact, he was not. They weren't trying to deceive me. The agency was misinformed at the time of my birth, and they simply passed that erroneous clue on to me. Be aware that anything you have been told may be incorrect. For this reason it is important to learn as much as you can to corroborate what you know.

DIRECTORIES OF DIRECTORIES

The American Library Directory and the City and Business Directories of the United States have already been mentioned as tools you can use to locate other resources. There are many, many others available to you, as well.

To begin with, the Guide to American Directories can help you find out if there is a specific directory which you should consult. There are directories of professions, for example. Almost every doctor in the country would be listed in the American Medical Association (AMA) Medical Directory. More information can be found for specialists in The Directory of Medical Specialists published by Marquis.

Other professions list members also. Books like the National Roster of Realtors or the Membership Directory of the National Society of Professional Engineers or the Directory of Women Entrepreneurs are extremely helpful if one of your birth parents (or grandparents) was a member of those particular professions.

Professional groups also license their colleagues. If you knew your birth mother or birth father (or grandparents) had been a lawyer, writing for a copy of their license could help lead you to them. How would you find the licensing bureau?

Most libraries have what is called the State Yellow Book. It looks like the yellow pages put out by the phone company, but instead it is a list of the current addresses of all 50 states' legislative and judicial branches, as well as many of the state boards. Any of these addresses can be helpful.

In the back of this book in the Subject Index is a heading for "Licensing - Occupational/ Professional". Addresses for State Boards which license in almost every profession - pharmacists, nurses, optometrists, doctors, building contractors, engineers, etc. - are listed in this section. Obviously, you could also locate these offices through the information operator in your state capital.

Another helpful source is the Business Organizations and Agencies Directory by Kruzas, Thomas, and Gill. This volume has addresses and phone numbers for colleges, state agencies, DMV's, major newspapers, diplomatic offices, business offices and information centers, lists of data banks, computerized services, and "information on demand" businesses.

For additional information on colleges, there are several other resource books like Lovejoys College Guide and Barron's Profiles of American Colleges.

Did your birth father attend a trade school? There is the American Trade Schools Directory which may help you narrow down where he attended school.

Was your mother Episcopalean? Want to know which churches existed in her home town? Obviously, you can look them up in a local phone book. But libraries also have directories of churches in their reference section like The Episcopal Church Annual and the Official Catholic Directory which will give you the names of the pastors and priests in residence at parishes throughout the country.

Do you want to contact a judge about opening your records but don't know who or where to ask? Check the reference section for the U.S. Court Directory which lists both courts and presiding judges.

Just for fun - what was happening on the day you were conceived? The day you were born? Facts on File Yearbooks give a day by day accounting of the news events which happen each year. It may not provide any clues to your mystery, but it helps to fill in your sense of your past.

Marquis publishes volumes and volumes on individuals every year in it's "Who's Who" books. There's more than just Who's Who in America and Who's Who in American Women. There's also,
Who's Who Among Black Americans
Who's Who in American Politics
Who's Who in Fashion
Who's Who in Entertainment
Who's Who in World War II
Who's Who Among Men and Women in Science
to name just a few. Obviously, not everybody's birth parent is going to be listed in one of these directories, but if you know your birth parent is involved in a particular profession, check to see if they are cited.

Did either of your birth parents have a hobby or an avocation that you are aware of? Were they stamp collectors, bowlers, bird watchers, or astronomy buffs? Perhaps your parents were informed of these interests during a casual conversation with the adoption agency at the time you were placed with them. Almost every hobby, sport, and pastime has an organization these days. Could your birth parent be listed among the members of such an organization? The Encyclopedia of Associations lists almost every such organization in the country.

Check the **GENEALOGY** section of your library. Books by genealogists on the art of searching can help you in your own efforts. The American Society of

Genealogists puts out volumes on genealogical research methods and sources. Other books like the Gale Genealogy and Local History Series (vol. 15, p. 233-35, by J. Carlyle Parker) can be extremely helpful, providing a bibliography on adoption searching, a list of search organizations, and other helpful aids.

The MORMON CHURCH is an excellent genealogical resource. The Church has several libraries across the country in which they have archival records on thousands upon thousands of people. Even if you are not of the Mormon faith, if one of these special libraries is accessible to you, by all means use it as a resource!

PHONE BOOKS

Libraries have phone books from around the country. Have a name to check and a location? Pull out a phone book and look it up. If the name you are looking for is Jane Johnson and you're looking in New York City, you'll obviously have pages of names to xerox. On the other hand, if you're looking for Zelda Kurzgowicz, your job will be much easier.

Let's say you don't know a location but you <u>do</u> have a very unusual last name like the one above. Look it up in every phone book your library has for the entire country.

Phone books will list area churches, locations of schools, numbers of local and state agencies, locations of organizations and businesses. Old phone books (or city directories) from the year when you were born may list phone numbers and addresses of **MATERNITY HOMES** or half-way houses where your birth mother may have stayed during the last part of her pregnancy. If the maternity home still exists, have they maintained any records on your birth mother? It's worth finding out!

The phone company will provide you with your own phone book of a specific region if you request it. If you are focusing your search in Tuscaloosa, Alabama, ask the phone company for a current phone book. It will be a resource at your finger tips and will save you long distance information calls or trips to the library.

Do you get the impression that you should spend a few hours/days/weeks at your local library? I hope so! As an easily accessible and welcoming resource center, it is one of the best places to spend your research time.

There are many other resources available to you other than those listed here. You will have many discoveries of your own about what your local library offers.

Enjoy your expeditions within its doors!

There are two books published by the U.S. government which your library probably won't have but you will find helpful:

Where to Write for Birth, Marriage, Divorce and Death Records (stock #017-022-01109-3) is available for $1.75 from the:

Superintendant of Documents
U.S. Government Printing Office
Washington, D.C. 20402
202-783-3238

The second book, the Guide to Genealogical Records in the National Archives, is available free from:

The National Archives
Washington, D.C. 20408
202-501-5402

SEARCH ORGANIZATIONS

There are many organizations which have been created in the last two decades to assist adoptees, birth parents, and adoptive parents in searches. Some are local in their scope, some national, some international.

Joining an organization can be very helpful. Interaction between all three members of the "adoption triangle" (adoptee, adoptive parent, birth parent) can lessen tension and provide understanding. Other searchers may have "contacts" or new suggestions which can help you in your search. And perhaps most important, these organizations can provide emotional support throughout your search. Friends and relatives might not understand your needs or motivations to search: other searchers will.

Some agencies provide a registry as a part of their organization. Many reunions have occurred because both an adoptee and birth parent register in the same organization and a match is made.

Two of the largest and better known agencies are ALMA (Adoptee's Liberty Movement Association) and CUB, International (Concerned United Birthparents). Their addresses are:

>ALMA
>P.O. Box 154
>Washington Bridge Sta.
>New York, NY 10033
>212-581-1568

>CUB
>2000 Walker Street
>Des Moines, Iowa 50317
>515-263-9558

There is a large registry know as SOUNDEX International which is also worth contacting because of the large number of names in it's registry. It works the same way as organizational registries. If both an adoptee and a birth parent register, then a reunion can occur.

SOUNDEX
P.O. Box 2312
Carson City, Nevada 89701

All these organizations keep their records completely confidential to protect the privacy of all three members of the adoption triangle.

For the addresses of other adoption agencies, perhaps a local one in your region, another organization may be of assistance: the American Adoption Congress. Primarily an international legislative organization which advocates access to records by members of the "adoption triad", the A.A.C. offers a free search referral service throughout the world. For more information on the services they have available call or write the A.A.C.

American Adoption Congress
1000 Connecticut Ave. NW, Ste. 9
Washington, D.C. 20036
1-800-274-OPEN

ADVERTISING

There are other places to advertise for birth parents outside of registering with an organization. By placing an ad in the classified section of a newspaper from your search area you may be able to have immediate and direct contact. An ad might read:

BIRTH MOTHER: DO YOU KNOW ME?
BABY GIRL SIMMONS
Born: SEPT. 9, 1948
County Hospital, Elmore, Virginia
Please reply: PO BOX 1, NY, NY 10000

Where should you place such an ad? In any local newspaper where you believe your birth mother or other birth relatives may reside. When? The best time might be the week of your birthday, every year. You can try at any time, of course, but many birth mothers think of their "birth children" on their birthdays. An ad like the above might catch a birth mother's eye more during this time.

There are specialty magazines where it might be useful to place an ad. For example, does your birth parent have a hobby? Does an organization he/she might belong to have a magazine or newsletter? Advertise there - it probably won't be too expensive.

Also, there are magazines like the new "Reunions, the Magazine" which have a section for people searching. Advertising there, just like registering with search groups, might help initiate a reunion.

Reunions, the Magazine
P.O. Box 11727
Milwaukee, WI 53211

PRIVATE INVESTIGATORS

Contrary to what I'd hoped and imagined, when I hired a private investigator she did not sneak into the adoption agency in the middle of the night and covertly photograph my file. But hiring an investigator eventually led me to my birth mother. An investigator can bring special methods of attaining information to aid in your search.

However, unless money is no object, I recommend pursuing every angle you can think of on your own first before using the services of an agency or individual. Why?

Two reasons: an investigator's time is expensive. Searches can easily run several thousand dollars (one agency estimated the average cost of a search in 1990 at $3500), particularly if you haven't done any footwork ahead of time. If an investigator is starting from scratch, piecing together your whole puzzle might take hundreds of hours (or one hour). It depends on the particular circumstances of your case. Secondly, because you are driven in you search, you won't give up easily. You are the most diligent and motivated investigator you can hire.

But after a period of months or years, you may run out of ideas and into dead ends. At that point, an investigator might be a tremendous help. If you do use an investigator, be sure up front about the fees to be charged. Also, request that the investigators provide you with a step by step synopsis of their efforts so that you know exactly what they have done and who they have contacted for your search journal records.

Private investigators are usually listed in the yellow pages of phone books under the heading

"Investigators". You may want to talk to several before proceeding with one. Two agencies with proven track records for locating birth parents are:

Tracer's (est. 1924)
Robert Eisenberg
Medford, Long Island, NY
212-558-6550

Klopper Investigations
Sheila Klopper
San Jose, California
408-243-8447

There are amateur investigators who may also be of help. Many list their services with local search groups or magazines. If you are unable to travel to an area where you are searching, this may be a less expensive answer to finding help. Many of these individuals have had great success in their own searches, and are willing for modest fees to do research for other adoptees. Again, check through the American Adoption Congress for search organizations and referrals.

PERIPHERAL CONNECTIONS:
Other People From The Past

Let's say you firmly believe you've located one of your birth parents or birth grandparents in a city directory from the year of your birth. How old are you right now? 25? 40? The trail is long cold. How do you find that person today?

Old landlords, employers, and neighbors may be a big help.

If you can find a former address of a birth parent, track them as long as possible through city directories. When the trail stops, go back through old city directories. Was their place of business listed? Does the business still exist today? Call information to see. Does an old employer remember this particular employee? Do they know what happened to them? Where they relocated to? If they married, do they know what their new name might have been? By chance, do they have old records on the employee? A Social Security number?

If you can't find an employer, how about an old landlord. Did your birth parent own the building they were living in? City directories often show if residents owned or rented a building.

How about old neighbors. Using the cross-reference section of a city directory, locate neighbors your birth parent might have had. Are any still at that current address today? Do they remember your birth parent? Do they know where they may have moved on to next? Had they married? Etc., etc.

This can be a very effective way of following a trail if you're lucky to locate someone who's been in a neighborhood a long time.

Another method of locating past acquaintances is to visit the neighborhood where a birth parent might have lived. Walk the street, drive around the area. Are there any corner stores that have been there for decades? Does a shop owner remember your birth mother? Her family? Do any tenants in homes or apartments near your birth parents old address remember them?

MILITARY RECORDS

Were either of your birth parents or grandparents in the armed forces? If you have their names, write a letter to:

The National Personnel Records Center
9700 Page Boulevard
St. Louis, Missouri 63132

Explain that you are a birth relative doing genealogical research, and that you can't locate discharge papers on this person.

For more information on how to track someone through military records, send for:

How To Locate Anyone Who Is Or Has Been In The
Military
P.O. Box 51433, Burlington, NC 27216
or call 1-800-999-8068

CHURCH RECORDS

For your own baptismal records, check the church of your faith in the immediate vicinity of the hospital where you were born. You are looking for a baptismal record listed by your birthdate which would have your original name on it, and the name of your birth mother.

For your birth parents you would do the same thing. Look for their records - either baptismal, marriage, or death - at churches in the vicinity of their birth or towns where you knew they had lived. Churches will generally catalog events of their parish by sacrament, and then by date.

**Churches are used to receiving requests from people doing genealogical research.

HIGH SCHOOLS AND COLLEGES

Your birth parents probably attended high school. It's possible that they went on to college. If you have an idea where they might have attended school, you might be able to locate them.

Local high schools, both public and private, generally publish a yearbook of their students every year. This often includes pictures, not just of the graduating seniors, but of every attending student.

Can you guess by what you know of either birth parent where they may have attended school and when they should have graduated? Remember to take into account the details of your own birth. For example, if your birth mother was 17 when you were born, she may not have graduated with her class or finished high school at all. Look for her as freshman or sophomore.

If possible, visit the school you believe they may have attended in person. Old yearbooks are often housed in either school libraries or in administrative offices. It's wise to call the school before making a special trip to make sure old copies of the particular yearbook you seek still exist.

Even if you don't have a name, a yearbook can lead you to a birth parent. Let's say you know a nationality and a physical description but have no name. Yet you are sure, vis a vis the process of elimination, that your birth parent would have attended a certain high school.

Go through the yearbook name by name for what you think would be the appropriate year. Pick out all individuals that have a last name that would seem to be of the correct nationality, be it Polish, English, German or whatever. (You would later cross reference those names against a book of name derivations.) Be sure to also check the year before and the year after (some students skip grades, others are held back or start later).

I know of a young woman who located her birth parents on the first day of her search simply by looking them up in a college yearbook. Obviously, it helps to have a name. But remember, you may greatly resemble the person you seek.

High school classes usually have reunions after ten or twenty-five years. There is generally a reunion chairman for each class. The administrative office of the school (or the school district if the school no longer exists) should be able to help you establish contact with the reunion chair. Ask for an updated address list of the entire class. This can be an extraordinary find. Even if your birth parent's name is not on the current list, you may be able to locate someone who knew her/him. Remember to be discreet. No one needs to know why you are trying to reach this person. Protect your birth parent's privacy.

College yearbooks and alumni lists are just as helpful as high school ones. The only drawback on yearbooks as a source is you usually need to see them in person, and for some searchers the necessary travel might not be feasible or practical.

THE D.M.V.

Government agencies keep track of almost all citizens for tax purposes and other reasons. Much of the information is difficult to access. For example, Census records from the years after 1910 are not open to the public. Passport and immigration paperwork is kept confidential for seventy-five years. But there are some government records which are easily accessible which can be quite helpful.

The Department of Motor Vehicles for most states will release information on licensed drivers. All you need to request this information is:

> the driver's full name
> and birthdate.

People frequently use the DMV to locate people who they have had an accident with, who they want to check on their safety record for employment purposes, and a variety of other reasons. Most states will send you a data sheet on a driver if you simply write a short letter formally requesting the information. A small fee may be required. The local DMV or the central office at the state capital can inform you of what you need to do for your particular state.

If you feel you're "zeroing in" on a specific person, these records can be enormously helpful. They provide not only a current address for the individual, but a physical description as well. If you know a few of the physical characteristics for the person you seek, this can help you to confirm whether you have the right individual. For example, you're looking for your birth mother, Jane Smith, and the adoption agency informed you that she had black hair, brown eyes and was five foot four. You believe a certain Jane Smith Johnson is the woman you seek. You request her driving records, and learn that Jane Smith Johnson is five foot nine with blond hair and green eyes. You know you need to look further.

Again, when you begin to zero in on specific individuals, it's important to try to learn as much as you can to confirm you have the right people. This can save on both embarrassment and grief, and protect individuals from accidental contact who have nothing to do with your past.

A PARABLE OF SEARCHING

The following bit of fiction is not about a real person, but it parallels real searches. It's purpose is to demonstrate how to put the tools we've discussed to use.

"Once upon a time, Emma North, a 27 year old adoptee, decided to search for her birth parents. Emma had had a happy childhood, yet had always been curious about her unknown past. Now that she was married and thinking of starting a family, her need know more about her genetic history was getting stronger.

So Emma decided to search. She began by contacting seven major sources - the people and organizations which surrounded the event of her adoption. She started a search journal to file all her gathered information in, and was full of hope in the first weeks of her search. But her hope waned somewhat after she began to receive little information.

Emma learned her delivery physician had died long ago, and the whereabouts of his records were unknown. The hospital where she was born sent her a copy of the medical records of her birth, but all the identifying information had been blanked out. She sent for her original birth certificate, but never received anything. Her parents couldn't locate the Final Decree, and the attorney they had used no longer practiced in the state. At this point, Emma talked to a superior court judge about opening her records, but he was unsympathetic. In fact, the only information Emma was able to retrieve was from her adoption agency. At the end of the first phase of her search, Emma's profile of her birth mother looked like this:

THE PROFILE CHART

?
_____
Name

?   Madera, Missouri
_____ _____
Birthdate   Birthplace

20   ?
_____ _____
Age at your birth
                           Last Known Address
Single
_____
Marital Status

Height: 5'5"   Weight: 120 lbs.

Eye Color: Brown   Hair Color: Blond

Religion: Lutheran   Race: Caucasian

Citizenship: U.S.
Nationality(s): Swedish_____

High School_____
Educational Background

_____?_____
Medical History

_____?_____
Military Service

Background History:_____?_____

_____
_____

Emma was disappointed initially, but when she created her Profile, she realized she had more information than she thought. There were still many sources she had not tried. With her husband's support, she decided to stick it out a while longer.

Emma was born in 1957. Knowing her birth mother was 20 at the time of her birth meant she must have been born in either 1936, 1937, or 1938. She knew her birth mother was born in Madera, Missouri. Using an atlas, she located the town. Questions began to enter Emma's mind. What was Madera like? What people lived there? Were any of the people she was related to still in that city? How would she ever find them if she didn't know their names?

Emma realized that she did know that the people she was looking for did live in Madera in the late 1930's. She checked the State Union List of Newspapers to find out what the local paper had been during that decade. She learned it was the Madera Gazette.

Emma checked with her local librarian and borrowed microfilm of the Madera Gazette through an interlibrary loan. She ordered records of the paper for every month from January 1936 to December 1938.

When the microfilm finally arrived, Emma began to search every paper. Her research was tedious and time consuming. But it allowed Emma to narrow the field. She meticulously looked through all the Madera birth announcements for a specific clue: Emma knew her birth mother was of Swedish extraction. She copied down the information on every name that appeared even remotely Scandanavian.

Emma ended up with a list of 37 names of baby girls born in Madera, Missouri between 1936 and 1938 who had Swedish sounding surnames. With her list in hand, Emma cross referenced every name against a book of name derivations to learn if it is of Swedish origin.

Nineteen of the names were Swedish. Emma now had a refined list of names. What next? She went back to the Profile of her birth mother. What else did she know about this woman? She was Lutheran. She finished high school.

Emma decided to travel to Madera herself to continue her research. She found out as much information as she could about the town ahead of time. There were two high schools in Madera, and one Lutheran church.

Emma's birthmother was 20 years old in 1957. Unless her education followed an accelerated pattern, she would have graduated from high school in 1954, '55, or '56. Emma learned that of the two high schools, only one had existed in the fifties: Madera High. She visited the school library. After locating yearbooks from those three years, Emma looked for any of the names from her refined list in the high school yearbooks.

As Emma went through the three annuals, she looked both for any women whose names were on her list, and if they were, did they match the physical description of her birth mother: five foot five, brown eyes, blond hair, 120 pounds. Emma left the library excited. Three women from the high school fit names she found in the birth announcements.

Emma moved on to the local Lutheran church. She explained to the pastor there that she was doing genealogical research. She asked to look through their register of records - the book within which baptisms, marriages, and deaths of the parishioners were recorded. The pastor of the church was very helpful.

Emma looked through the years 1936 to 1939 seeking baptismal records of any of the names from her list, most particularly the three names that matched in the high school yearbook. Emma copied everything down in her journal. While Emma found four names from her original list of 37 who were baptised, none of the 3 from her high school list were listed.

Emma returned home feeling perplexed and depressed. Trying to find seven people by names they probably no longer went by seemed impossible. Then, five weeks after her return, Emma's mother called her. In going through a box of papers in the attic, she had located Emma's Final Decree. Emma now had her original name: Dana Ann Swensen.

When Emma heard this name over the telephone, she was ecstatic. One of the three high school girls had a last name Swensen. She pulled out her search journal, and looked up the name. Wisely, she had made a xerox of the picture. The young woman's name was Danika Swensen. Emma had a rush of feelings as she sensed she was perhaps looking at her birth mother for the first time.

But where was Danika Swensen now? Who had she grown to be? Had she married?

From the birth announcement in the Madera Gazette, Emma now knew Danika's birthdate was July 1, 1937, and the names of her birth grandparents were Ingrid and John Swensen. Emma tried to locate city directories or old phone books at the local Madera library, but had no luck. The town was too small for a city directory, and the library housed only current phone books. But in talking with the Madera librarian, Emma learned that a Madera Historical Society existed. Emma called them long distance and found they did have old phone directories. John Swensen had lived at 314 Maple Drive. Emma then realized she had not tried current information for John Swensen. She called information only to learn there was no one listed by that name in either Madera or the surrounding towns. Emma asked for listings of all the Swensens that did live in Madera.

At this point, Emma could have called all the Swensens in the book to see if any of them knew Danika Swensen or her parents. Or she could have gone through years of old phone books to see when John Swensen disappeared from the listings, and then I looked for an obituary in that period of years for him. But instead, Emma decided to see if Danika had married sometime between when she was 20 and 25. She called the pastor she had befriended at the Lutheran church. Even though there had been no baptismal record of Danika as a child, she still might have married in the church. Emma chided herself for not having checked marriage and death records while in Madera.

The pastor willingly checked the records. If he had been unsuccessful at finding any marriage record, Emma was ready to make a request through the county recorders office for a search of any marriage records for a Danika Swensen, child of John and Ingrid Swensen, born on July 1, 1937. But this proved unnecessary. When the pastor called back he told Emma that Danika Swensen had married in the church in 1957. Her husband's name was Erik Johannsen. The pastor had taken the initiative to check the local listings. An E. and D. Johannsen lived in the neighboring town of Alderville.

Emma's long search was coming to a close. She now needed to decide the best way to contact her birthmother. Perhaps the pastor could help..."

Every search is unique. Some will take a minimal effort. Others will be a great struggle. Emma's search lies somewhere in between. This fable proves a point. Emma's Profile of her birth mother may have seemed a weak foundation, but she actually had enough information to open the door to several other clues. Persistence pays off. So does time. So does ingenuity.

THE REALITY OF YOUR OWN SEARCH

In my own search, I had little more to go on than Emma. Yet, after narrowing down numerous ambiguous clues, I ended up with only one name that seemed to fit. And as amazing as it seemed to me at the time, I had actually found the right person.

Emma's story has the ending that every searching adoptee desires: a full resolution. That's certainly what I hoped for at the end of my search. Answers. But what about your own search? What if you reach a dead end at every turn? What if your trail disappears after years of gathering information? What if everything you try from this book doesn't lead you anywhere?

You may find many people are not receptive to helping you. Wait a month, or a year. Try again. There are many stories of searchers who never take "no" for an answer, who call a source back again and again hoping that someday they will learn a piece of the truth. So try again. Maybe someone new will be running the hospital records department and will be sympathetic to your cause. Maybe someone will make a "mistake" and give you access to records you were previously denied. Maybe a different judge will feel you have a right to your records. Times are changing. People are slowly beginning to understand the strong need adoptees have to discover their roots. Ultimately, this may result in changes in state laws. But until that day arrives, active searching will be the only way to make a reunion happen.

Winston Churchill once said, "Never, never, never, never give up." This philosophy is a life attitude which searchers must adopt. Almost anyone who has ever pursued this quest has faced frustration, anger, and despair. On those days when it seems that you've tried everything, pull out your journal and go through it one more time, page by page. Is there one more clue you can pursue? Is there anything from the Search Checklist at the back of this book that you haven't tried? One more stone to turn?

You may find times when you simply need to stop your search for a while. Take some time off. SEARCHES ARE DRAINING. There are invariably ups and downs. Try to anticipate them. Join or create a support group to help you through the different stages of your search.

Your search may take a day (you should be so lucky) or a year or a decade. The reality is, some searchers are never able to locate anyone. There are those who give up trying after the first set-back. Others give up trying after they have tried everything.

If this is your fate, to search without ever locating your roots in person, try not to despair. Your search for the "holy grail" - your origins - has been a search for truth. I believe if you do everything suggested in this book you will learn something about your roots. You will know at least part of the truth. This enhancement of self-knowledge, while incomplete, is worth every moment you have devoted to your search. And perhaps, the fact that you have tried against all odds to pursue this quest tells you as much about yourself as anything else you will ever find.

The following poem was written by an adoptee who finally decided, after years of searching, to let go.

"Genetic roots....
It seems that I may never
learn who they are
or what they were.
I may have to settle
alone
for what I am
and have always been.
And maybe that's for
the best.
I may end
Where I began
More an original weave
Than a thread
from a patterned
Tapestry."

P.S. Two years after this searcher gave up, she found her birth parents....

WHEN YOU FIND SOMEONE....

Try to picture this day.

You have a telephone number in your hand. It belongs to your birth mother. What will you do with it? Have you considered the way in which you will first establish contact?

Preparing for a reunion is something you need to do throughout your search. What do you anticipate from a reunion with birth parents?

Think it through. Try to visualize dozens of different outcomes, from the worst to the best, and imagine how you would handle each situation. This can help you be somewhat prepared for the vast spectrum of possible scenarios that could result from your search.

Your birth parents may no longer be alive. They may reject you. They may be overwhelmed by your arrival. Or they may be completely overjoyed at being found. Perhaps they will have expectations of their own. How would any of these situations make you feel?

Preparation is important. But no matter how prepared you are, no matter how many scenarios you try to anticipate, the reality is that it is impossible to forecast how your birth parents will react - or how you will react.

Anticipate that no matter what the results are, you all will have a period of adjustment. The initial joy of a reunion can melt into awkwardness. It takes time to establish these new and unique relationships.

A NOTE TO BIRTH PARENTS....

This book is primarily a resource for adoptees who are searching. Used in "reverse", however, it becomes an excellent resource for birth parents too.

Use this book to know <u>where to leave clues</u>.

Contact the adoption agency and sign a Waiver of Confidentiality so that if your birth child files also, the agency knows you want to be located. Contact the hospital, the delivery physician - everyone the adoptee may contact - and let them know you would welcome a reunion.

Keep your eye out for ads in newspapers. Make sure you're listed in phone books and city directories. Tell the courts you want to be reunited.

Register with search organizations.

Advertise yourself in magazines and newspapers.

Your birth child may never search, but in case he or she does, if you want to be found, leave a "trail of bread crumbs" to follow.

THE SEARCH CHECKLIST

PHASE ONE

HAVE YOU....

____ 1. CREATED A SEARCH JOURNAL? See page 7.

____ 2. Discussed the search with your
parents? Had them sign a Waiver
of Confidentiality? See pages 10-11, 14-15.

____ 3. Located your amended birth
certificate? See page 16.

____ 4. Retrieved a copy of your Final
Decree? See pages 12-13.

____ 5. Retrieved a copy of your Petition
to Adopt? See pages 12-13.

____ 6. Contacted the agency which handled
your adoption? See pages 21-24.

____ 7. Contacted the law firm or the
specific attorney which assisted in
your adoption? See page 25.

____ 8 . Contacted the physician or mid-wife
who delivered you? Asked he/she to
assist you by requesting medical
records from the hospital? See pages 17-18.

____ 9. Filed a Waiver of Confidentiality
with the adoption agency, the law firm, and
the courts? See pages 14-15.

HAVE YOU....

____ 10. Attempted to retrieve your original
birth certificate? See page 26.

____ 11. Applied for the medical records from
the hospital where you were born?
See pages 27-28.

____ 12. Personally contacted a judge about
opening your records? See pages 30, 52.

____ 13. Formally petitioned the courts to
open your adoption records? See pages 29-30.

PHASE TWO: PROFILING EVERY PERSON YOU SEEK

PHASE THREE: CROSS-REFERENCING

____ 14. Checked the county recorder's office to
see if your original birth certificate
is on file? See page 19.

____ 15. Checked records (both county and state)
for divorce and annulment records
for either birth parent? See pages 47-49.

____ 16. Researched copies of the adoption
laws for your state? See page 29.

____ 17. Checked local (county or state) death
records for birth parents or
grandparents. See pages 47-49.

HAVE YOU....

____ 18. Written the Adoption Regulation Unit
to access adoption records. See page 13.

____ 19. Sent for a copy of <u>Where to Write</u>
<u>for Birth, Marriage, Divorce and Death</u>
<u>Records.</u> See page 56.

____ 20. Ordered a copy of the
<u>Guide to Genealogical Records in</u>
<u>the National Archives.</u> See page 56.

____ 21. Attained a copy of a map or maps for
the areas where you're searching?
See page 40.

____ 22. Created a profile of the home towns or
regions where each of your birth
parents were to have come from?
See pages 41-42.

____ 23. Created a list of all the libraries in
your area and in the localities where
you are focusing your search? See page 34.

____ 24. Checked local newspapers from the area
where you were born for birth
announcements. See pages 43-45.

____ 25. Checked local newpapers from the area
and era when your birth parents were
born for their birth announcements?
See pages 43-45.

____ 26. Checked local newspapers for wedding
and engagement announcements for your
birth parents? See page 45.

HAVE YOU....

_____ 27. Checked obituaries in local newspapers
where you believe your birth parents
may be from for notices of either
their own death, or the death of a
birth grandparent? See pages 45-46.

_____ 28. Checked in old city directories to
try to locate birth parents? See pages 36-39.

_____ 29. Checked in city directories to match
an occupation to a name? See pages 37-38.

_____ 30. Checked in city directories for former
(or current) employers of birth
parents? See pages 36-39.

_____ 31. Cross-referenced city directory
information year by year? See pages 36-39, 62.

_____ 32. Checked in city directories to locate
old addresses and possible neighbors?
See pages 36-39.

_____ 33. Checked old and new phonebooks in your
local libraries for possible past and
current locations of birth parents
and other relations? See page 55.

_____ 34. Requested copies of phone books for
your target searching areas. See page 55.

_____ 35. Checked old phone books for listings
of all churches of the faith of your
birth parents in the area where they
were located at the time of your
birth - and now? See page 55.

HAVE YOU....

_____ 36. Cross-referenced any possible surnames
against a book of name derivations?
See page 50.

_____ 37. Checked local churches in the area
near the hospital where you were born
for any baptismal records? See pages 52, 64.

_____ 38. Checked local churches in the area
where you believe your birth mother
or birth father may have resided for
records of baptism, marriage, or
death? See pages 52, 64, 72-74.

_____ 39. Joined a local or national search
organization and registered your birth
date with them? See pages 57-58.

_____ 40. Registered with SOUNDEX
International? See pages 57-58.

_____ 41. Advertised in adoption search
magazines and newsletters? See page 59.

_____ 42. Advertised in newspapers where you
believe a birth parent might now live
to try to locate them? See page 59.

_____ 43. Applied for your birth mother's and
birth father's original birth
certificate? See page 26.

_____ 44. Located any maternity homes or halfway
houses that existed in the area of
the hospital where you were born
at the time of your birth? See page 55.

HAVE YOU...

_____ 45. Contacted the Department of Motor
Vehicles in the state where you
believe a birth parent may reside to
locate current addresses and confirm
identities? See pages 67-68.

_____ 46. Contacted old landlords for forwarding
addresses? See pages 62-63.

_____ 47. Contacted old neighbors for forwarding
addresses and other information?
See pages 62-63.

_____ 48. Visited old neighborhoods in person
to locate past acquaintances. See page 63.

_____ 49. Checked with former employers about
possible forwarding addresses of
birth parents? See pages 62-63.

_____ 50. Checked old high school and college
yearbooks? See pages 65-66, 72-73.

_____ 51. Checked with a high school or college
reunion chairman about the current
address of a birth parent - or requested
a list of the entire class? See pages 65-66.

_____ 52. Checked with professional licensing
agencies for copies of licenses if
birth parents or grandparents who have
professional backgrounds? See pages 51-53.

_____ 53. Contacted a hobby club or other
organization you believe a birth
parent may belong to? See page 53, 57.

HAVE YOU....

_____ 54. Applied for military records for both
birth parents? See page 64.

_____ 55. Sent for a copy of <u>How To Locate Anyone
Who Is Or Has Been In The Military</u>?
See page 64.

_____ 56. Checked the archives of the Mormon Church?
See page 54.

_____ 57. Contacted a private investigator?
See pages 60-61.

_____ 58. Checked the Genealogy section of the library
for additional search methods? See page 53.

_____ 59. Checked "Who's Who" resources for specific
professions that relate to your birth parents.
See page 53.

_____ 60. Contacted the American Adoption Congress
to use it's free referral service?
See page 58, 61.

If you have any questions or need
further assistance in your search,
feel free to contact me directly.

I wish you all the best in your
efforts - if you're successful,
I'd enjoy hearing your story!

Jean Strauss
"The Great Adoptee Search Book"
P.O. Box 161
Worcester, MA 01602